AF574740

A Source Book of World War 2 Weapons and Uniforms

A Source Book of

World War 2 Weapons and Uniforms

Frederick Wilkinson

Ward Lock Limited · London

First published in Great Britain in 1980
by Ward Lock Limited, 116 Baker Street,
London W1M 2BB, a Pentos Company.

House editor Suzanne Kendall

Layout by Jude Fletcher

Text filmset in Univers
Set, printed and bound in Great Britain by
Fakenham Press Limited, Fakenham, Norfolk

British Library Cataloguing in Publication Data

Wilkinson, Frederick
A source book of World War 2 weapons and uniforms.
1. Uniforms, Military – History – 20th century
2. Arms and armor – History – 20th century
3. World War, 1939–1945 – Supplies
I. Title
355.1'4'09044 UC480

ISBN 0–7063–5898–8

Acknowledgments

The author and publisher would like to express their sincere thanks to the staff of the Imperial War Museum for their help in preparing this book. Thanks are also due to Paul Forrester who took a number of the photographs, including the jacket picture.

Frontispiece. Gurkhas from Nepal – many of these fine soldiers fought with the British army. They are wearing standard battledress and steel helmets fitted with camouflage netting. The one on the left has a Thompson sub-machine gun with a box magazine and the others have Lee Enfield rifles.
Imperial War Museum

Introduction

World War I ended in November 1918 with the defeat of the Central Powers by the Allies. For the beaten nations such as Germany and Austria times were very hard and many people offered ideas as to how things could be improved. In Germany during the early 1920s an ex-corporal Adolf Hitler became leader of a small party known as National Socialists, Nazis for short. He was a powerful speaker who persuaded more and more people to support him and by 1933 he had become the leader, or Chancellor, of Germany. Soon he was in complete control of the country and was known as the Führer.

In Italy another leader, Benito Mussolini was in total command and before long the two dictators had agreed to support each other in every way. Their union was known as the Axis.

Hitler was very anxious to make Germany powerful and strong and he began to build up the army, navy and air force. Mussolini was also keen to see Italy as the ruler of an empire and in 1935 the Italians invaded Abyssinia (now Ethiopia) in Africa. In the Far East Japan had ideas of ruling an empire of her own and supported Germany and Italy.

In 1936 Hitler made his first move and sent his troops into the Rhineland which was under the control of the French. To his delight the French did nothing and Hitler felt that he could now try something even bigger and in 1938 he claimed Austria as part of his kingdom, or Reich. A little later he began to call for part of Czechoslovakia to be put under German rule. Britain and France persuaded the Czechs to agree to his demands and then in March 1939 Hitler took over the rest of Czechoslovakia.

It was clear that sooner or later France and Britain would have to take some action. When Hitler began threatening the Poles both countries warned Germany that any attack on Poland would lead to war. Hitler did not take the threat seriously and laid his plans and on 1 September 1939 he ordered the attack. The Allies (Britain and France) called on the Germans to withdraw or they would declare war and this they did at 11 a.m. on 3 September 1939 and World War II had started.

The Poles fought hard, but the Germans' clever use of their tanks, aircraft and infantry working together, soon defeated them and within three weeks they had to surrender. Their defeat was hastened by the fact that Russia also invaded the

country and in November 1939 Russia also attacked Finland. The small, but valiant Finnish army fought so well that it was not until March 1940 that they admitted defeat.

In Britain and France nothing seemed to be happening and many people felt that the Allies were not really trying to defeat Germany. Very little happened until early 1940 when the Allies considered plans to stop supplies reaching Germany; these entailed some action involving Norway. The Germans were aware of the plans and in April 1940 they invaded Denmark and Norway. The Allies sent troops to help the Norwegians but they were badly equipped, the planning was poor and they were unable to do much good.

The Germans were now ready for the main attack and early on 10 May 1940 they stormed into Holland and Belgium although both countries were neutral. British and French armies moved north into Belgium to hold the Germans but they were ill-prepared and the planning was bad. German tanks smashed their way through the Allies' lines and swept round the

Although poison gas was not used during World War II troops carried respirators and here a German soldier wears his for practice. The Alsatian is carrying a message and is equipped with his own respirator.
Imperial War Museum

end of the Maginot Line which was a long line of forts and strongholds designed to protect the French frontier. Soon they had reached the Channel coast and cut off the Allied armies in the north. On 28 May the Belgian army surrendered and many of the British and French armies were left isolated and surrounded. A fighting retreat enabled them to reach the port of Dunkirk and a great armada of small ships sailed across the Channel from Britain to rescue the troops. Despite very heavy losses the ships managed to bring back nearly 340,000 troops to England.

In the meantime the Germans swept on from victory to victory and on 22 June 1940 France surrendered leaving Britain to fight alone.

The Germans now prepared to attack Britain and plans were made to launch an invasion across the Channel to land on the south-east corner of England. Before this audacious plan, code-name Sea Lion, could be undertaken it was vital that the Germans should gain control of the air. The Luftwaffe, under the command of Hermann Goering, was ordered to smash the R.A.F. Heavy raids were launched against airfields and every effort was made to destroy the British fighters. Air battles went on throughout July, August and September but the Luftwaffe was unable to defeat the R.A.F. The British had two good fighters, the Hawker Hurricane and the Supermarine Spitfire and they were helped by radar which was a radio device which let the British find German planes when they were as much as 240 km (150 miles) away. This gave the British fighters plenty of time to get into position ready to attack. By October the Battle of Britain was over and Operation Sea Lion had been postponed. During much of the Battle of Britain many British towns, especially London, were heavily bombed.

In June 1940 Italy declared war on the Allies who then decided that an attack would be launched against that part of North Africa ruled by Italy. Throughout the latter part of 1940 and early in 1941 the Italian army suffered greatly at the hands of the British under General Wavell but in February 1941 Adolf Hitler sent troops under the command of one of his most able generals, Erwin Rommel, to support the Italians. These troops, known as the Afrika Korps, inflicted heavy defeats on the British and drove them back. They were helped by the fact that the British troops had been reduced in numbers. On 28 October 1940 Mussolini had invaded neighbouring Greece but despite his hopes of a quick victory the Greeks fought back bravely and defeat looked sure for the Italians. British troops from North Africa had been sent to help the Greeks and Germany again stepped in to help out her ally. By the end of April

1941 almost all organized fighting in Greece was over and the British were forced to withdraw.

Hitler's carefully worked out timetable had been sadly upset by the need to support his Italian allies who were proving to be almost more nuisance than they were worth. Hitler had, throughout the whole of 1940, been planning his greatest operation and on 22 June 1941 he launched against Russia one of the largest armies the world has ever seen. The operation, code-named Barbarossa, was well planned and Hitler was sure that it would succeed. His generals did not expect much opposition from the Red Army which they believed to be poorly equipped and badly officered. However Barbarossa had been delayed by the need to send troops to help the Italians in Greece and although the German army swept on to some magnificent victories they were gradually slowed by the heroic resistance of the Russian army. By the end of the year they were short of their objectives and suffering from the terrible Russian winter for which they were unprepared.

In the meantime Rommel, in North Africa, was also suffering defeats and being slowly pushed back but in 1942 he began a massive counter-attack and began to drive back the British from all the territory that they had captured.

On 7 December 1941 the Japanese navy and air force launched a surprise attack on the great American naval base at Pearl Harbor in Hawaii. The attack was a tremendous success and the Japanese inflicted heavy casualties, sinking many warships. At the same time they attacked British and American possessions in the Pacific. As a result of the Japanese aggression America joined Russia and Britain and all three soon began to make plans for the defeat of Germany – Russia was not then at war with the Japanese although she did declare war on them at a later date. The three leaders of the Allied countries, Winston Churchill, Franklin Roosevelt and Josef Stalin, met several times during the war to decide policy and draw up plans.

The Japanese seemed invincible and swept on through the whole of December taking Hong Kong, landing in Burma, Borneo and the Philippine Islands forcing the Americans and British on the defensive. The British and Americans agreed that their first task would be to finish the war in Europe and then set about defeating Japan. In January 1942 the first American troops began arriving in the United Kingdom, they were called G.I.s because their uniforms were marked 'Government Issue'.

German horse-drawn supply wagons making their way through heavy mud during the 1940 French campaign.

Throughout the whole of 1942 the Russians and Germans were engaged in tremendous battles with enormous losses, and in the Philippines, despite some successes by American and British naval forces, the picture looked very black as the Japanese seemed to sweep on to more and more victories. However the great power of the factories and arsenals of the United States was beginning to make itself felt as fresh supplies rolled across the Atlantic and Pacific. Delivering these supplies was not easy because the German submarines, U-boats, sank many of the ships and in order to leave as much room on the ships as possible for war supplies, food, clothing, petrol and many other things were rationed.

Another important feature of 1942 was the increasing strength of British bombing raids on Germany. Raids on German targets were made from the beginning of the war but the early ones carried only leaflets calling on the Germans to stop the war but as the fighting increased so bombs replaced the leaflets. In May 1941 the big bomber raids began but at first bomber crews often lost their way or missed their target and the results were very disappointing. However the introduction of big, new, four-engined bombers like the Lancaster and the Halifax and the development of new devices made it possible for the crews to find their way in total darkness and bomb accurately even through thick cloud. Despite the greater accuracy and heavier raids the bombers, R.A.F. by night and US air force by day, did not manage to stop German production of essential war supplies.

During the latter part of 1942 the tide of war began to change and after a battle beginning on 23 October at Alamein in North Africa, the German and Italian forces began a great retreat. In November 1942 a large American and British force landed in North Africa behind the German lines, to attack the Italians and Germans. By the end of May 1943 the Axis forces had surrendered and all of North Africa was in Allied hands.

The Allies now began their attacks on the European mainland and in July 1943 they invaded Sicily. In September the Italians signed an armistice but this did not mean the end of fighting in Italy for the Germans had brought in troops and they continued to fight against the British and Americans.

In the Pacific Japan was beginning to suffer defeats and plans were already in hand for an Allied leap-frog attack on the mainland of Japan. The idea

Finnish girls supporting the army against the Russians in 1940. On the front of their fur caps they have the Finnish lion.
Imperial War Museum

being that Japanese-held islands would be occupied in turn until, eventually, the British and Americans would have bases close enough to Japan to launch an attack on the mainland.

In Russia events were turning against Germany as they tried to hold fierce Soviet attacks but lost heavily, especially at Stalingrad in January 1943. At Kursk the greatest tank battle ever fought also ended in defeat for the Germans. In 1944 the Russians were advancing on all fronts.

In Italy the Germans managed to hold most of the Allied attacks but in the meantime the R.A.F. by night and the US air force by day continued their intensive bombing of German industry, ports and supply centres. On 6 June 1944 Overlord, the long-expected invasion of Europe by the Allies, began. By many clever tricks the Germans had been led to believe that the main attack would come in the Pas de Calais area which was closest to Britain but, in fact, the attack was launched on Normandy. The offensive was a great success although the fighting was very heavy and the Germans, under pressure on both their Russian and European fronts, were gradually pushed back. In Italy the British and US forces had nearly cleared the country of Germans and in October 1944 British troops landed in Greece. In the east of Europe the Russians had reached Czechoslovakia and liberated most of Poland.

These are some of Italy's Colonial troops, or Askaris, from Libya. The soldier on the right is cleaning the barrel of a Breda machine gun – this gun fired 8 mm cartridges at a rate of 475 rounds a minute but it was a poor design and not at all popular with the troops.
Imperial War Museum

Not all the Allied attacks were successful and one tragic defeat was that of the British Airborne offensive at Arnhem in September 1944 when, because of a series of unfortunate coincidences, the Germans held the attack and the British Airborne Division suffered very heavy losses. Although victory was in sight the Germans were by no means defeated and in December 1944 they launched a massive attack against the US army in the Ardennes in the south-west corner of Belgium. The US forces were completely unprepared and the Germans made great advances, sweeping forward in what became known as the Battle of the Bulge. In January 1945 the German Luftwaffe launched a tremendous attack on Allied air force bases, again achieving complete surprise and inflicting very heavy losses. After some very fierce fighting the Germans were forced back and the battle won.

In the east the Russians were continuing their pressure, they captured Warsaw, the capital of Poland in January 1945 and kept up a relentless advance. By the February they had captured Budapest in Hungary. As the Russian and Allied armies moved nearer to each other the Germans fought on bravely. They also continued to use their flying bombs, V1s, and rockets, V2s, to bomb Britain and other parts of Europe. Berlin was captured by the Russians and in an underground shelter, The Bunker, Hitler and other leading Nazis killed themselves. At 1201 hours on 9 May the European War officially ended.

Although the European War ended with V.E. day, that against Japan was still very much alive. The Allied forces had been driving their way across the Pacific, bombers were raiding Japan inflicting tremendous damage and it looked as if the mainland would soon be invaded. However the Allies had been working for many years on a terrifying new weapon, the atom bomb, which did not use ordinary explosives but the tremendous force generated when the tiny particles known as atoms were split

This sword with a gold inscription on the blade and a blue leather scabbard was a presentation piece from the leader of the German air force, Hermann Goering.
Sotheby & Co.

apart. On 6 August 1945 the Americans dropped the world's first atomic bomb on the Japanese town of Hiroshima. It virtually wiped out the town and on 9 August they dropped another one on Nagasaki and the Japanese realized that they could be totally destroyed. On 14 August the Japanese Emperor ordered the surrender of all his forces and V.J. day brought the end of the Second World War.

The cost in human life had been enormous and, although it can never be known for sure, the total number of those who were killed or died of their wounds was over 12 million. Although Germany lost $3\frac{1}{2}$ million it was Russia with a probable $7\frac{1}{2}$ million that suffered worst of all.

One big difference between World War I and II was the number of civilian casualties, for all those countries engaged in the war suffered air raids and in the United Kingdom alone nearly 150,000 civilians were killed or wounded; in Germany something over a million people were either killed or wounded. Many other civilians were killed during the years of fighting.

The Forces

When war began Germany had the best equipped, best trained and most efficient army in the world. France had a very large army but it was not well equipped and, in many ways, was weak and ill-prepared. The French commanders were convinced that the long line of underground forts, the Maginot Line, would keep out the Germans and much of their planning was based on this idea. When the German tanks, parachutists, motor cyclists and mobile infantry moved rapidly through their positions they lacked the skill and training to deal with them. Britain's army was really very small but was, on the whole, well-trained and equipped.

The Japanese had a large army, well-trained and, most important, prepared to fight to the death for they thought that capture by the enemy was far worse than death. They were able to live off the country and manage with far less equipment than western troops. The Italians were poorly led and generally, although by no means always, fought with little spirit. Their equipment was often rather poor.

When Germany conquered many of the countries of Europe and parts of Russia they had to fight a rather special enemy – the Resistance or Underground. Many very brave men and women risked their lives fighting the Germans by destroying railways, damaging telegraphs, helping people to escape, discovering secrets and passing them on to the Allies. Many were caught, tortured, imprisoned or executed but hundreds fought on. In France some hid in the wild countryside and were known as the Maquis, in Russia and Eastern Europe they were known as partisans or guerrillas.

The navies of the Allies fought only a few big battles and most of their time was taken up with hunting U-boats, shelling enemy positions for landing troops and guarding shipping. Aircraft carriers became much more important than battleships. German battleships such as the *Bismark* were superb and among the best in the world and their U-boats did so much damage to Allied shipping that they came near to winning the war for Germany.

The German air force started the war as a support force for the army and the dive bomber, Stuka 87B, played a very important part in smashing the Polish, French, Belgian and Dutch armies. During the Battle of Britain the dive bombers suffered heavy casualties and were withdrawn from the fighting by the Germans. The two main fighters, the Messerschmidt ME 109 and the Focke Wolfe FW 190 were very good indeed, in some ways better than the British Spitfire and Hurricane. Germany never developed big bombers but they produced some very advanced weapons such as the V1s and V2s.

The British R.A.F. had some good fighters and heavy bombers which concentrated on night bombing and Bomber Command suffered heavy casualties. The United States air force grew stronger and stronger as the war progressed and their big bomber was the four-engined Flying Fortress.

The Uniforms

Although the many forces wore different uniforms there were some similarities especially in choice of colour. The British were among the first to adopt khaki, a brownish, yellowy colour, but many other armies followed their choice, Belgium, Bulgaria, Czechoslovakia, Denmark, France, Greece, Hungary, Japan, Poland, Romania, Russia, United States, Canada, Australia, New Zealand all had khaki as their main colour although some had light and some had dark shades. The second most popular army colour was greyish green which was used by China, Germany, Italy, Netherlands and Norway.

The majority of designs were the same, with a tunic to the thigh, straight trousers and boots. The British wore a blouse-type garment which fitted closely to the waist and had many pockets as did the trousers. This design was known as battledress.

From 1940 onwards Germany suffered greatly from air raids most of which, until the US air force joined in, took place at night. The German air defences included many searchlights which were controlled by radar.
Imperial War Museum

Some, like the German and Romanian infantry wore jackboots which were about the size of wellington boots. Many officers of all armies wore jackboots. Other troops like the French, Dutch, Bulgarian and others wore puttees – long strips of cloth wound round the lower part of the leg and ankles. The British had short anklets which strapped on around the ankles.

Most armies had a light cloth cap, with or without a peak, which was worn all the time except in battle. British troops changed during the war to a beret. In the African campaigns the German Afrika Korps also wore a kind of sun helmet and it was very common for all those serving in the desert to wear a mixture of

issue uniform, captured enemy clothing and personal choice pieces. In battle these cloth caps were replaced by steel helmets which all had some form of inner lining and a metal outer part. When the first US soldiers arrived in Britain they were still wearing a British pattern helmet but in 1941 they began using a new, rather complicated pattern which consisted of a light plastic helmet which could be covered by a thick steel bowl. Tank crews often had protective helmets designed to be worn inside the cramped space of a tank. Airborne troops usually had specially designed steel helmets and often wore an overall which went over all their equipment.

Special uniforms were designed to be worn in certain kinds of country – white overalls for snow, light shirt and shorts for the desert. Camouflage became very important and sometimes troops wore net covers over their helmets and pushed leaves and twigs into the net so making it difficult for them to be spotted from the air. There were also special camouflage jacket and trousers with green and brown or sandy patterns which helped the soldier to blend into the background.

British armoured car designed for reconnaissance. Note the special hoods on the headlights and the Bren gun mounted on the small turret.
Imperial War Museum

All the forces had badges on their uniforms which showed such things as rank, trade or the special service the man or woman served in. The British and US army officers carried rank badges on their shoulder straps, and the sergeants and corporals and others wore theirs on the upper part of the sleeve. In the German and other armies collar badges were used to show the service. Many armies had special cap badges to show their regiments. British and American troops also had cloth formation badges which were worn at the shoulder. Many troops who escaped from their own countries when they were overrun by the Germans joined the British and they wore the name of their country embroidered at the top of the arm of their tunic.

Many air forces had the aircrew or flyers wear badges above their left breast pocket. In the R.A.F. they were of cloth whilst those of America were metal. Many air forces favoured a rather light blue coloured uniform and in the R.A.F. rank was shown by rings around the cuff of the tunic.

The infantry of all armies carried a whole range of equipment such as ammunition, bayonets, spare clothing, water bottles and respirators. These items were fitted on to a number of belts, straps and packs which usually fitted round the waist and passed over the shoulders.

The Weapons

When the war began the majority of infantry were armed with a magazine, bolt action rifle –

Britain – Lee Enfield
Italy – Mannlicher-Carcano
France – MAS 1936
US – M1C (Garand)
Germany – Mauser
USSR – Mosin Nagant
Japan – Arisaka

Officers usually carried a handgun –

Britain – Webley .455 or .38 Revolver
Germany – 1908 Luger or Walther P38 automatic
France – 7.65 automatic
Italy – Beretta 1934 automatic
USA – Colt .45 automatic
Japan – Nambu automatic

As the war went on troops used more and more automatic weapons such as sub-machine guns which fired pistol cartridges at a high rate. Some, like the British Sten gun, were very simple and cheap to make and were dropped by parachute to resistance groups.

Britain – Sten gun
Germany – MP 40
Italy – Beretta 9 mm
US – Thompson M3
USSR – PPSh 1941

Grenades were used by both sides, sometimes thrown by hand or else discharged from a rifle. They were very effective against tanks which played a big part in the war. Special weapons were designed for infantry to fight against armoured vehicles – the Germans had the *Panzerfaust*, the British had the PIAT – projectile infantry anti-tank, and the Americans had the bazooka.

Mines were buried just below the ground surface and exploded when something heavy rolled or trod on it. Some were made so that if anyone tried to lift them out of the ground they exploded.

Bayonets were carried by most troops but were little used in battle although very useful for opening tins, digging holes and for hanging things on.

Although not really intended as serious weapons, most German officers and leaders carried a dress dagger or sword. The pattern worn varied from service to service and there were changes in details.

Poison gas was held ready by many of the fighting nations but was never used during World War II; the troops all carried gas masks or respirators just in case.

Mortar

Mortars are used by the infantry as a kind of light artillery and throw small shells high into the air with a maximum range of about 1.5 km (1 mile). This is an American M2 mortar which fires a shell of 60 mm diameter (approx. $2\frac{1}{4}$ in). The barrel is a metal tube and is aimed by altering its angle of tilt. One G.I. is dropping the shell down the barrel and as it hits the base it will be fired out to its target.
Imperial War Museum

Rocket Launchers

The US bazooka AT M1, a two-man weapon firing a small rocket. The man at the rear is feeding in the 2.36 in diameter rocket. It was first used in North Africa in 1943.
Imperial War Museum

World War II saw a great development in rocket weapons and this is a 114 mm ($4\frac{1}{2}$ in) launcher mounted on a jeep – a very useful, general purpose vehicle. It fired 12 rockets at 2-second intervals. Note that the US soldier is armed with a revolver instead of the usual Colt automatic. The second G.I. has armed himself with a captured German bayonet. *Imperial War Museum*

The Russians made great use of their small rockets fired in salvoes from batteries, fixed or mounted on the backs of lorries. This photograph was taken at Stalingrad in January 1943. *Imperial War Museum*

Grenades and Bombs

Left: US M II A2 rifle grenade.
Centre: British M 36 M with base plate fitted so that it could be fired from a special rifle fitting.
Right: Russian F1 grenade – the sides are deep cut to ensure that the body would split into pieces.

Top left: Italian M 35 grenade.
Top right: Japanese mortar bomb type 89 – this was fired from a simple tube known as a knee mortar.

Bottom: British 76.2 mm (3 in) bomb for Mk 5 mortar; these were given an extra charge to increase their range – up to 2,400 m (2,600 yd).

Sub-Machine Guns

British infantrymen in New Guinea. The one on the left is armed with an Australian-made Owen sub-machine gun which fired 9 mm bullets at a rate of 700 rounds per minute. The other is holding his Bren gun which was officially adopted by the British army in August 1938. It is a splendid machine gun, accurate and reliable, firing a .303 bullet at a rate of 500 r.p.m.
Imperial War Museum

A Russian PPD 1940 G which was probably first used in 1938. It has a drum magazine holding 71 rounds of 7.62 mm cartridges. The inside of the barrel is chromium plated to reduce wear and prolong its life. The design was changed in 1940–41 and this sub-machine gun was replaced by the PPSh 1941 G. *Pattern Room, Royal Small Arms Factory, Enfield*

This is the famous Tommy-gun – designed by Colonel John Thompson in 1919. It was altered in detail and the 1928 model was probably the most common after it had been made simpler and was then known as the M1 (1942). The M1 was used by many of the Allied troops and could be loaded from a drum or box magazine (20, 50 or 100 rounds). *Pattern Room, Royal Small Arms Factory, Enfield*

Because of the great demand for new weapons many new, cheap, simple-to-make sub-machine guns were designed. In Britain the Sten gun was introduced in 1941 and several different patterns were made. The bottom gun is a Mk V Sten produced in 1944. Most Sten guns had a magazine which held 32 rounds of 9 mm. The Germans copied the Sten and were planning to issue the weapon to their secret underground fighters at the end of the war.

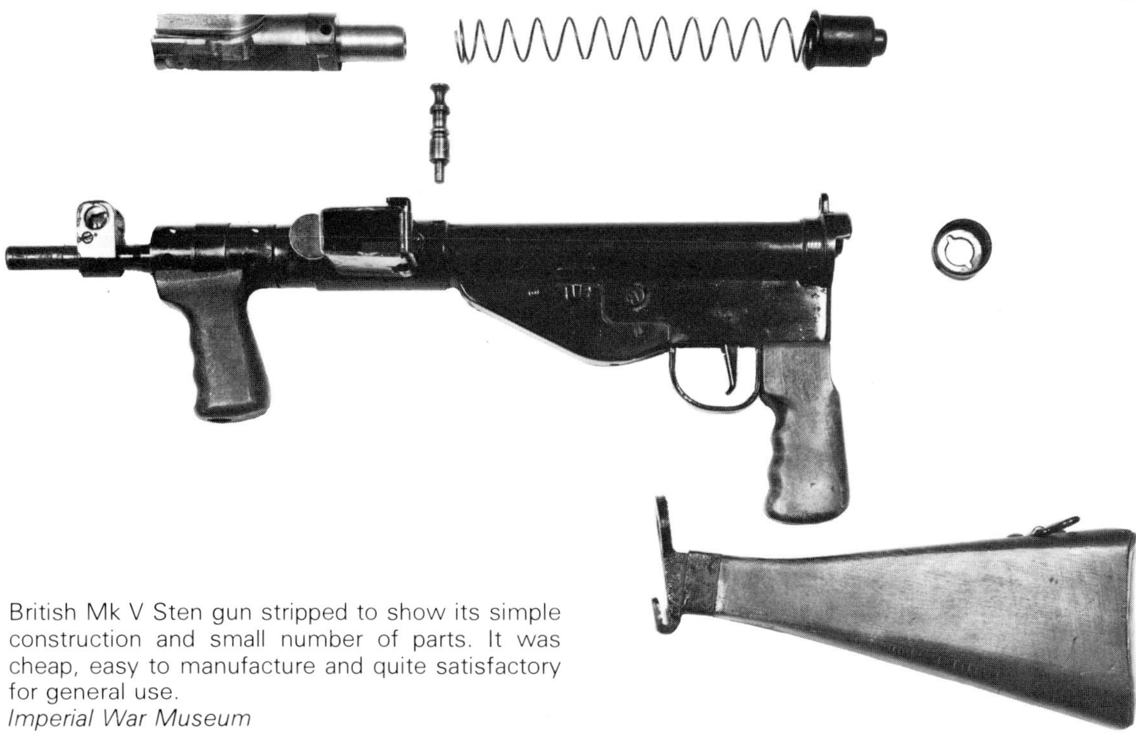

British Mk V Sten gun stripped to show its simple construction and small number of parts. It was cheap, easy to manufacture and quite satisfactory for general use.
Imperial War Museum

Top: US M3, a cheap, easily made .45 sub-machine gun with a rate of fire of 450 rounds a minute.
Middle: Russian PPS M 1943, a 7.62 mm sub-machine gun firing at a rate of 650 rounds a minute. It has a curved magazine fitting beneath the barrel.
Bottom: Italian Beretta M 38A 9 mm sub-machine gun with folding bayonet – a particularly fine weapon.

Top: German Bergmann MP 34 9 mm sub-machine gun.
Middle: German Bergmann MP 28II 9 mm sub-machine gun.
Bottom: Japanese Type 100 8 mm sub-machine gun.

Machine Guns

Designed by Colonel Lewis, this light machine gun was introduced in 1917 and continued in service through much of World War II although officially it was replaced by the Bren gun in the British army in 1938–9. It fired .303 cartridges fed in from a 47 round drum magazine.

Pattern Room, Royal Small Arms Factory, Enfield

US Browning M 1917 .30in machine gun. The rounds were fed in from a long, fabric belt which held 250 rounds. The barrel, as on all machine guns, became very hot and was cooled by water held in the tin and fed through the rubber tube.
Pattern Room, Royal Small Arms Factory, Enfield

German MG 42 7.92 mm machine gun. This general-purpose weapon had a very high rate of fire, around 1000 rounds a minute. It was very good and so was used for many purposes including anti-aircraft fire. The rounds came in metal belts of 50 rounds, which could be clipped together in multiple units to increase efficiency.
Pattern Room, Royal Small Arms Factory, Enfield

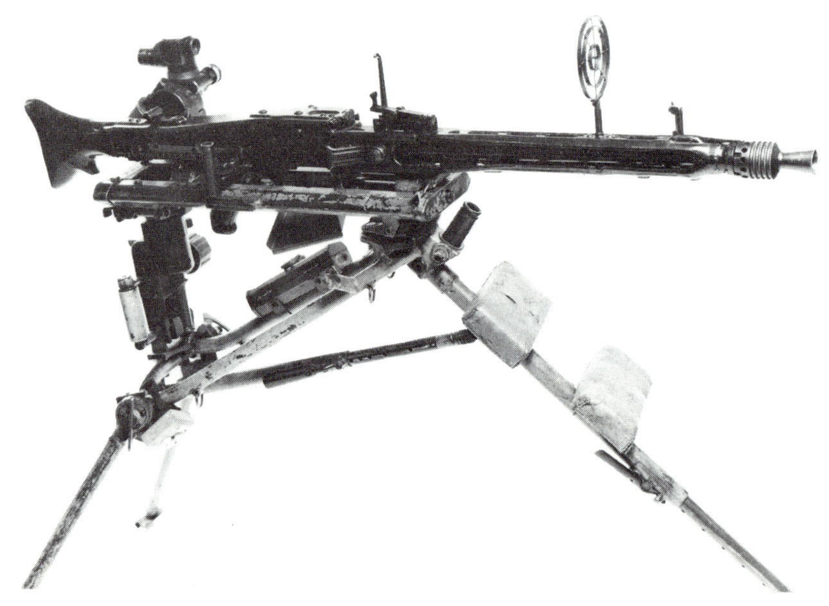

British, Vickers heavy machine gun saw service in World War I and II. The .303 ammunition was supplied in long fabric belts holding 250 rounds and the barrel was cooled by water contained in a drum around it.
Pattern Room, Royal Small Arms Factory, Enfield

Danish Madsen 7.92 mm machine gun which was used by the Norwegian army among others, and later by the Germans. It had a fairly slow rate of fire, around 450 rounds a minute.
Pattern Room, Royal Small Arms Factory, Enfield

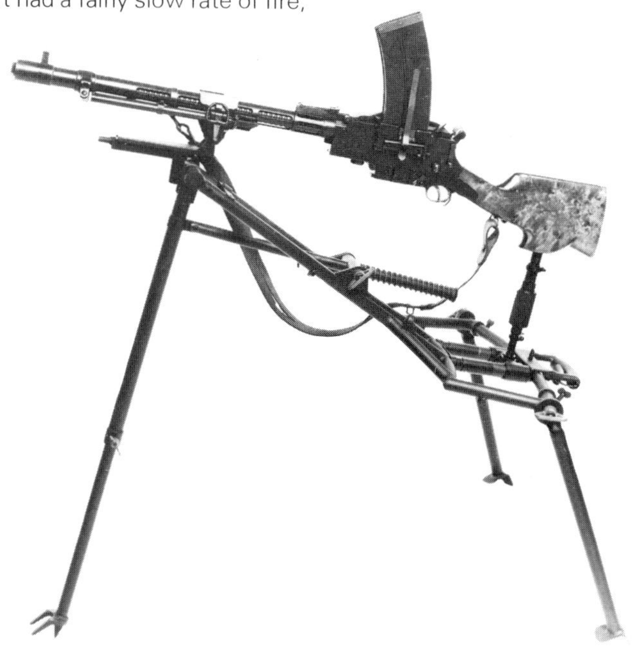

Revolvers

Top: British Mk IV Webley revolver – six shot – .455 calibre.
Middle: French Lebel revolver Model 1873 – still used in World War II.
Bottom: Russian Nagant 7.62 mm revolver – introduced in 1895 and manufactured right through to World War II.

Pistols

Top to bottom:

1 The famous Luger '08, 9 mm automatic – although replaced in 1938 it was still used by many German troops through World War II.

2 Walther P 38 automatic pistol 9 mm – officially adopted by the German army in 1938 – a very rugged and reliable weapon.

3 Polish Radom 9 mm pistol – one of the strongest automatic pistols.

4 Japanese Nambu automatic type 14, 8 mm pistol – ugly and poorly made.

Signal or flare pistols – used for lighting up the ground, signalling aircraft take-offs or ordering attacks or retreats.
Top: British No. 4 Mk I.
Middle: US 1942 Mk 5.
Bottom: German *Kampfpistole*.

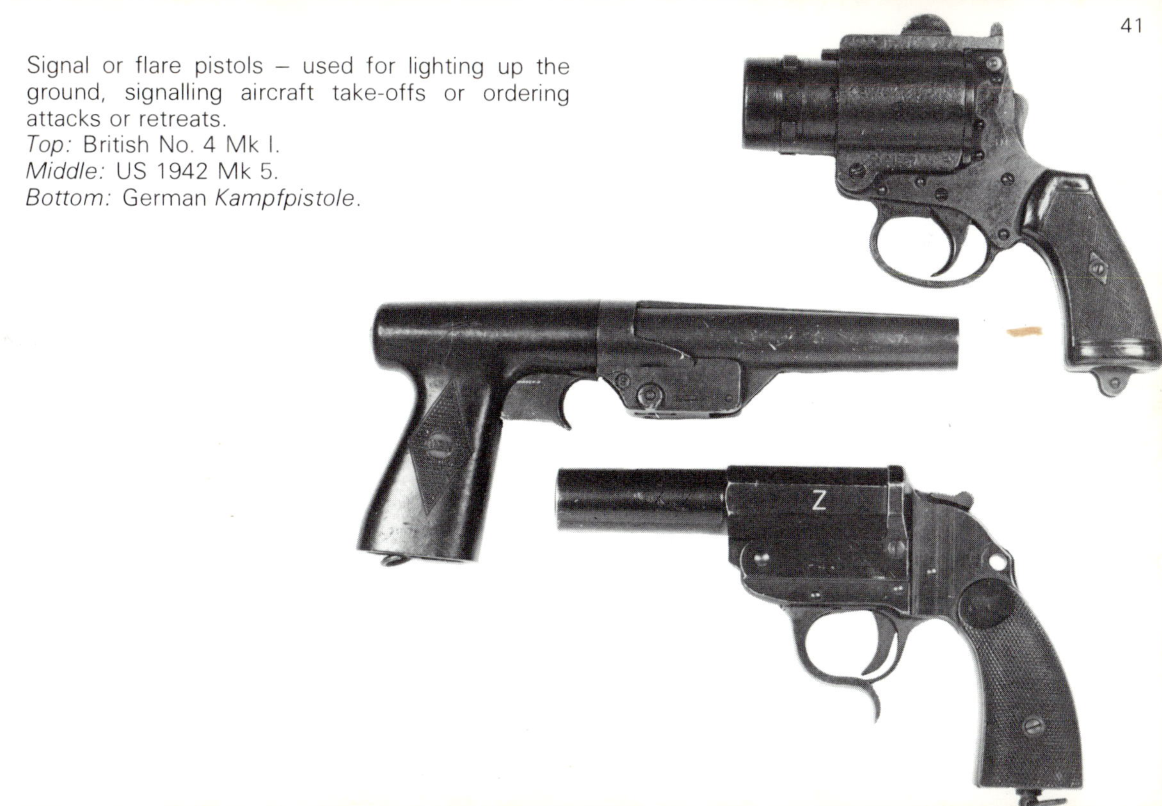

Rifles

US Browning automatic rifle M 1918. This was designed to be fired from the hip or shoulder but it was rather heavy and difficult to control. The box magazine held 20 rounds of .30 cartridges. Some of the models were fitted with tripods and carrying handles.

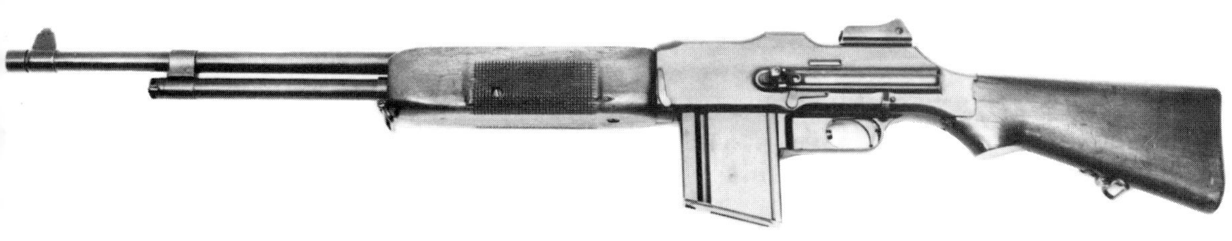

Top: British Short Magazine Lee Enfield rifle Mk III, .303 calibre. This weapon was later replaced by the Mk IV but was still in service with some units until the end of the war. This one has a webbing sling.

Middle: American Garand rifle, calibre .30 – this was loaded by an eight round clip and was a gas-operated, repeating weapon.

Bottom: French MAS 1936 rifle, 7.5 mm calibre with five round magazine.

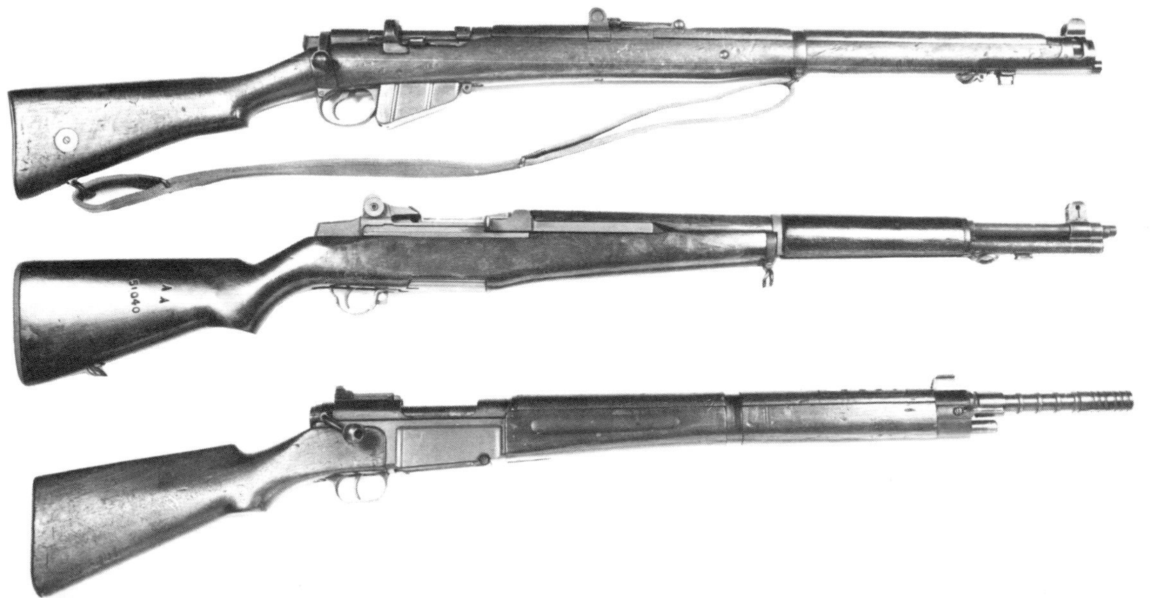

Top: Russian Mosin Nagant Carbine M 1944, 7.62 mm calibre – it has a permanently attached folding bayonet. *Middle:* Italian Model 91, 6.5 mm rifle. *Bottom:* Japanese Arisaka Model 30 rifle.

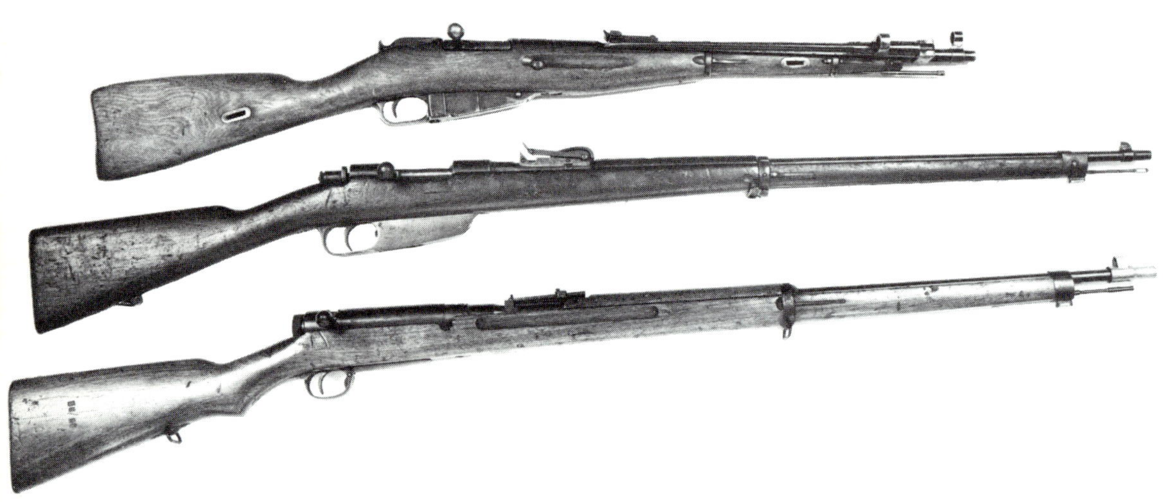

Italian rifle (Mocheto) Ballia, made for training young boys – it was special 6.5 mm calibre and would not fire ordinary cartridges.

Boys anti-tank rifle firing a .55 in calibre bullet and issued to British infantry from 1939. It was a heavy weapon with a very powerful kick making it unpleasant to fire.

German assault rifle Mkb 42(W) designed for a smaller cartridge than that of the standard rifle. Less than 8000 of this model were made but they saw service in Russia.

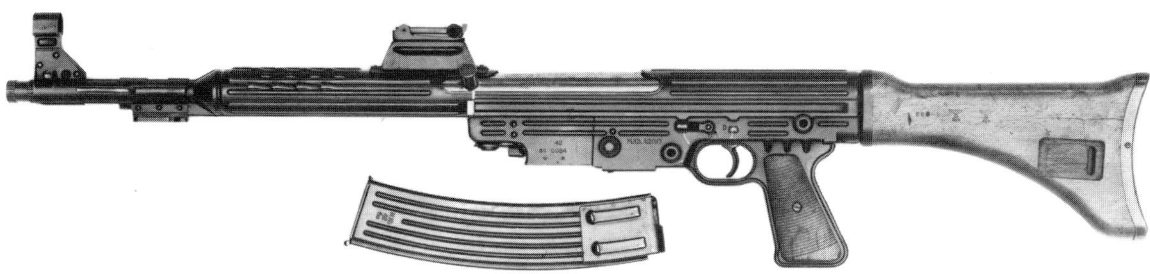

US bolt action rifles.
Top: M 1917 .30 calibre rifle originally designed to fire the British .303 cartridge, it was later changed to take the American cartridge – largely used as a training weapon.

Bottom: Springfield M 1903 .30 calibre rifle with a built-in, five round magazine. This weapon was replaced quite early in the war by the M1 Garand rifle.

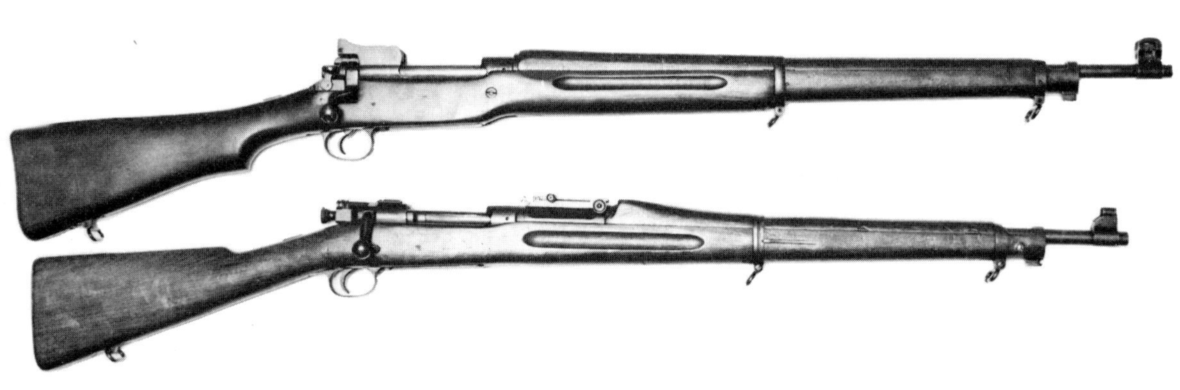

When the war began in 1939 many troops were still armed with the weapons of World War I (1914–18). Although newer models were supplied to the front line troops these older weapons continued to be used by reserves and for training.
Top: British Short Magazine Lee Enfield .303 rifle with a 10 round magazine – later replaced by a simpler version known as the Rifle No. 4 Mk 1.
Middle: German Mauser type 98 rifle with magazine for five rounds of 7.92 mm cartridges.
Bottom: French Lebel Model 1886 rifle with an eight round magazine for 8 mm cartridges.

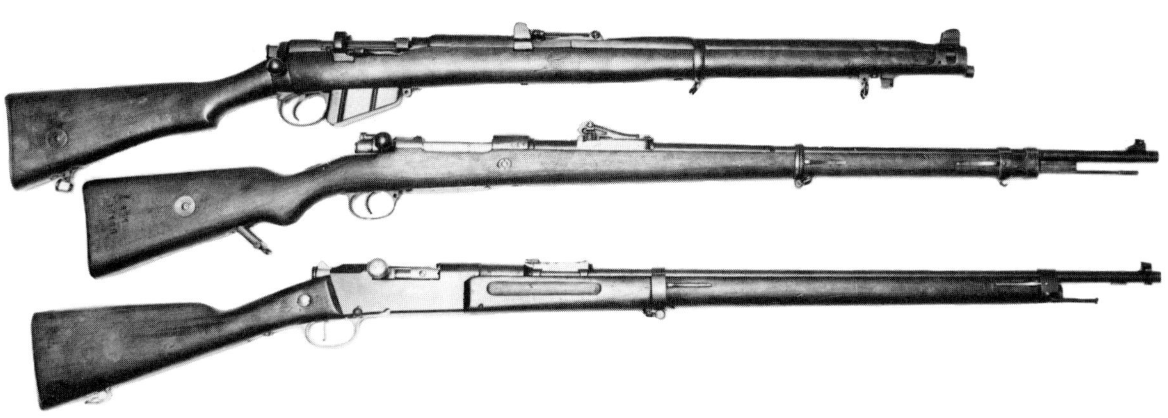

Bayonets

Dutch bayonet M 1895 for the Mannlicher rifle. This version is known as the Cavalry pattern and the leather sheath has a retaining strap fitted to hold the weapon safely in place.

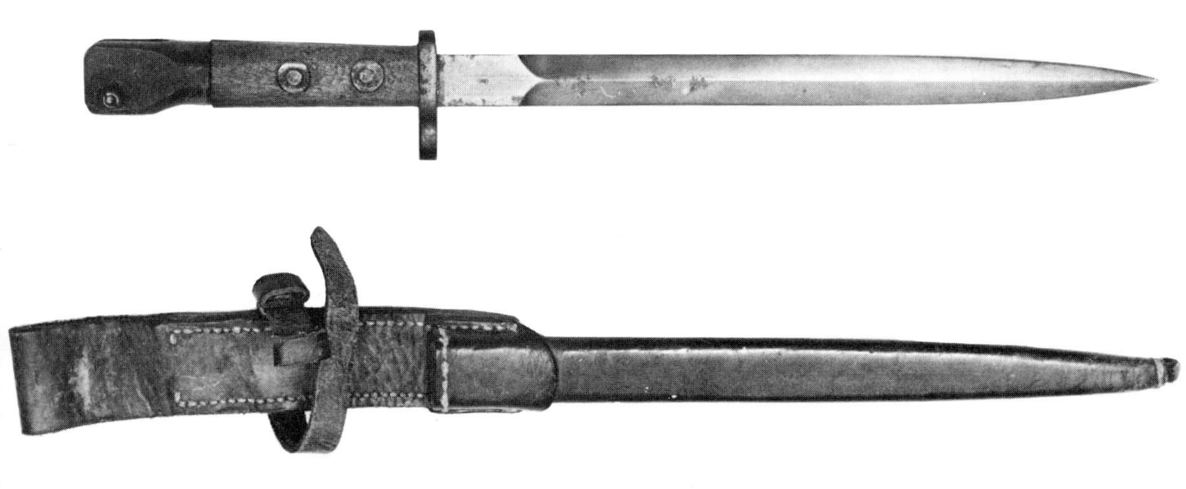

British P 1907 bayonet for the Short Magazine Lee Enfield rifle with its long, single-edged blade. This was later replaced by the shorter models.

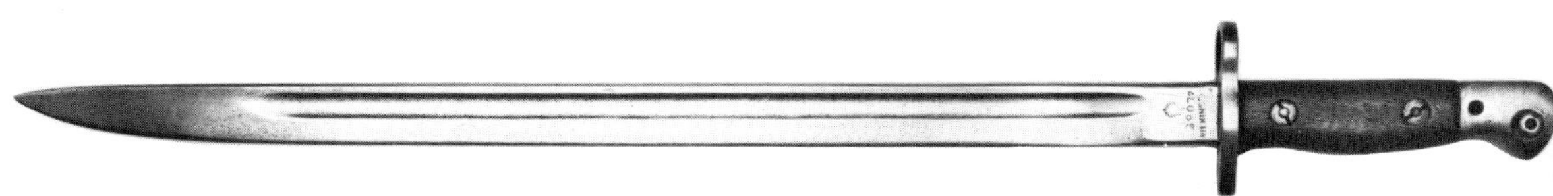

A new pattern rifle, the No. 4 Mk 1 was introduced early in the war and with it came a new style of bayonet. The original long blade was replaced by a short, ribbed one and later by a spike.

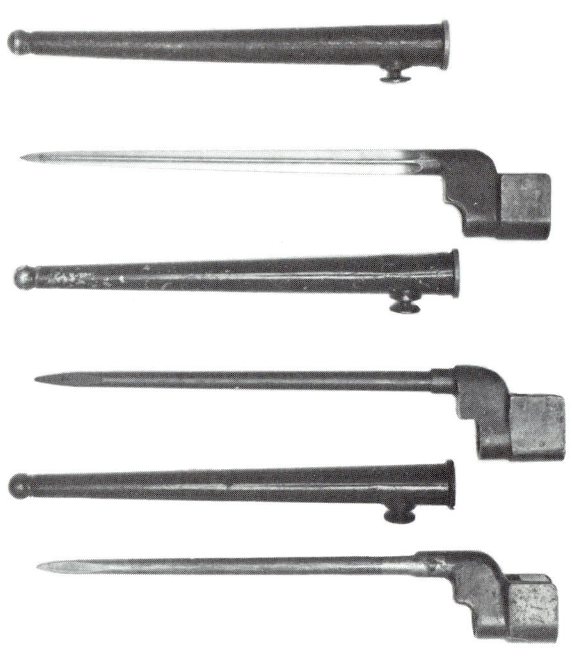

Top: British No. 4 Mk II bayonet – several patterns of this weapon were produced but all were very similar.
Centre: German model 84/98 bayonet for the Mauser rifle.
Bottom: French bayonet for the Lebel rifle – it was unusual in that the blade is cross shaped.

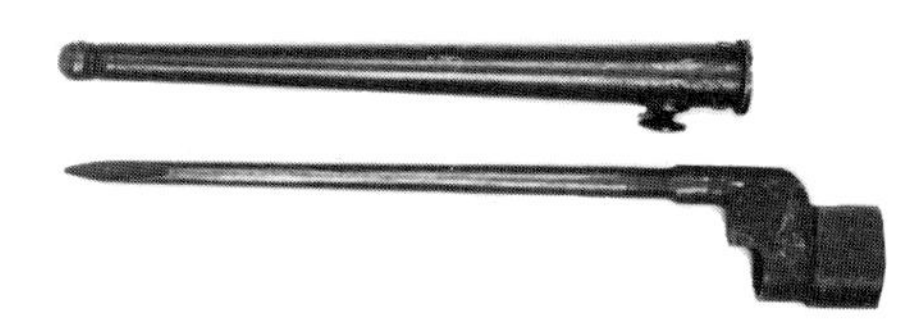

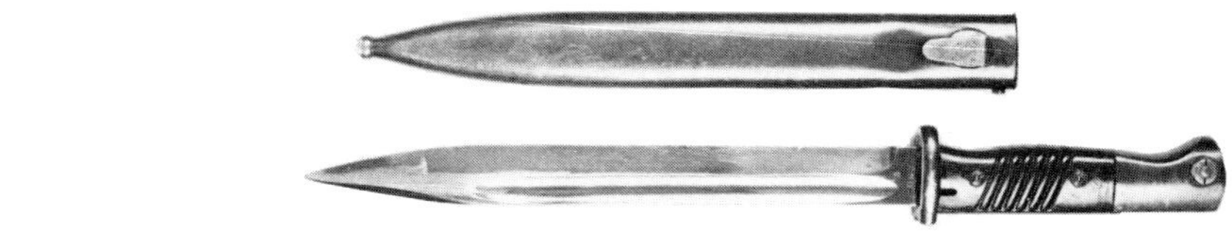

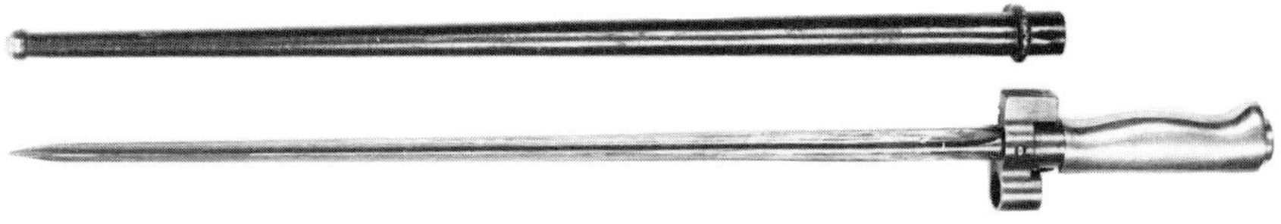

Top Russian Mosin Nagant bayonet.
Centre: US M1 1943 bayonet for the M1 Garand rifle or the M 1903 Springfield rifle.
Bottom: Bayonet for Japanese Arisaka rifle.

Daggers

Dress dagger worn by officers of the German Luftwaffe. It was hung from the belt by the double strap. Officers in the army, navy and other services had different patterns.
F. J. Stephens

This is the dagger which was worn by an officer in the German SS or *Schutzstaffel*. This unit was first formed to serve as a bodyguard for Hitler but it later became far more important, controlling its own armed forces and police.
F. J. Stephens

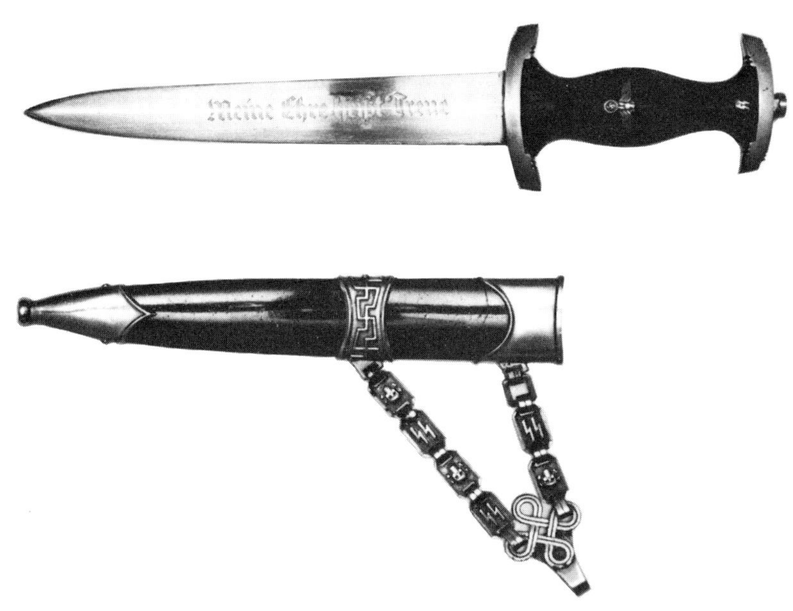

Knives

Top: British fighting knife carried by the Commandos, specially trained troops used for raiding the enemy. The leather sheath was designed so that it could be carried in a number of different ways.

Bottom: German Utility knife made to be opened in one hand, releasing the catch allowed the blade to fall into position. It was issued to parachute troops.

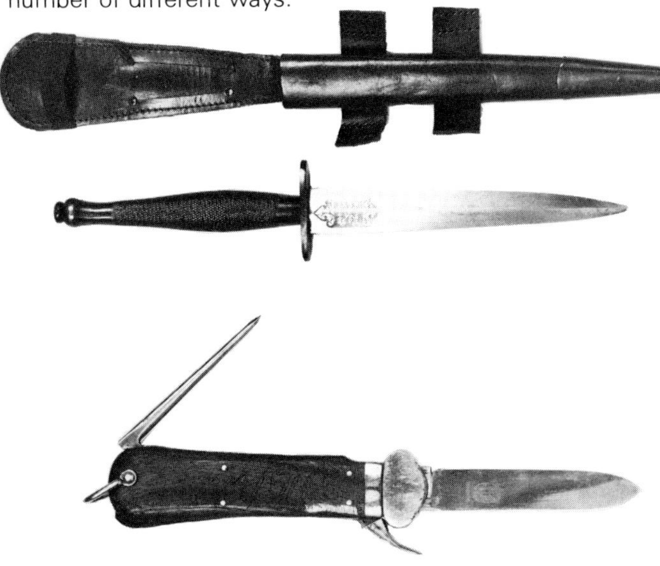

The Gurkhas from Nepal used all the modern weapons but they always carried their special knives – the *kukri*. The heavy blade was sharpened on the inside curve and was carried in a leather sheath. Many Gurkhas believed that once drawn the *kukri* could not be sheathed again before it had drawn blood.

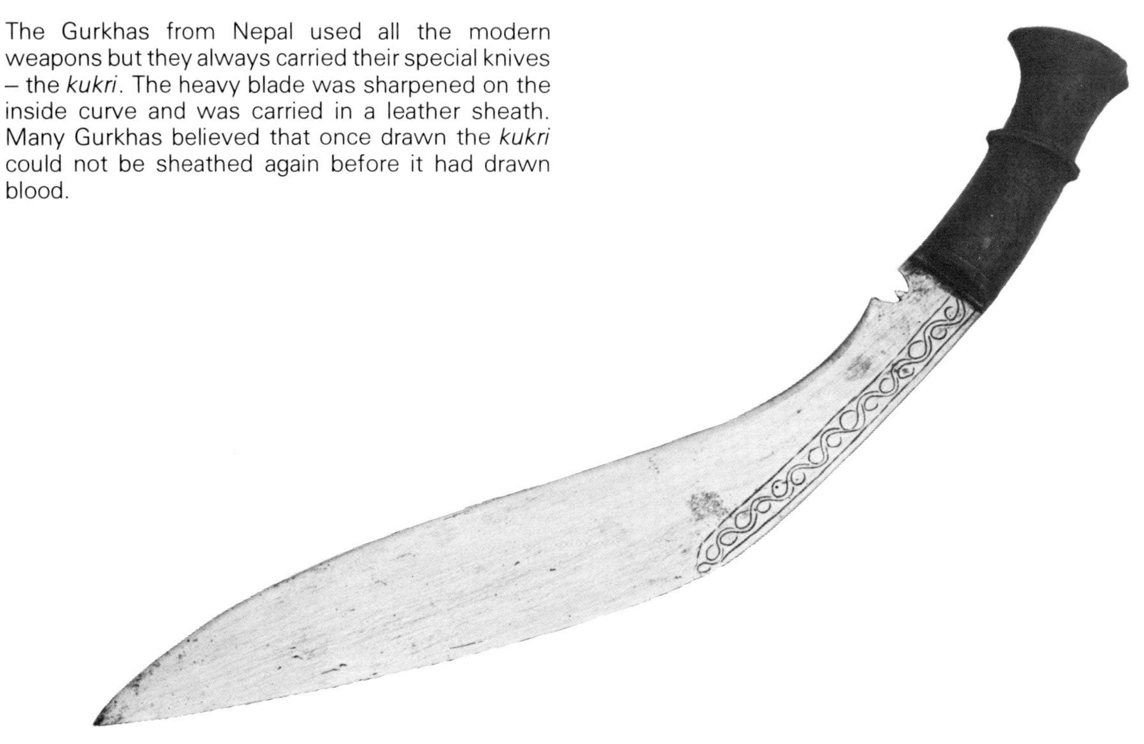

Ammunition

Left to right:
.32 (7.65 mm) ACP for small automatics such as the Hungarian P37.
9 mm Parabellum for Luger, Walther and many others.
.38/200 for British revolvers.
.45 ACP for Colt automatics.
.455 for Webley revolvers.
.30 M1 Carbine.
7.92 mm German service rifle.
30/06 for US service rifle.
.303 for British SMLE rifle.
.50 Browning heavy machine gun.
1 in flare cartridge.

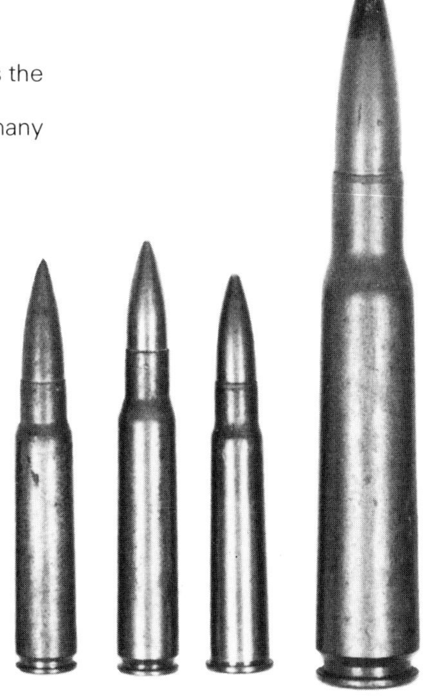

German Troops

The German soldier crouches by the side of a tank – probably the Pz Kw 111 Ausf J. He carries full field equipment including his gas mask in the cylindrical can, a water bottle just below and an entrenching tool in its leather carrying case.
Imperial War Museum

A German infantry officer at Stalingrad. On his tunic he wears an Iron Cross, a Wound Badge and a Close Combat Clasp. One of his men on the left is carrying a Russian sub-machine gun.
Imperial War Museum

German paratrooper (*Fallschirmjäger*) – he wears a steel helmet and holds his static line which was clamped to a rail in the plane. As he jumped clear the line opened his parachute at the right moment. He is an N.C.O. (*Gefreiter*), with one stripe on the arm. *Imperial War Museum*

Most parachutists wore special helmets and this one was used by the German airborne troops. The chin-straps were designed to make sure that the helmet was not easily knocked off the head when the parachutist landed.
Martin Windrow

The German army made great use of motor cycles and most were made by the firm of Mercedes. Many were fitted with a sidecar often with a machine gun mounted on the front. Motor cyclists were issued with special waterproof coats which could be hooked up between the legs for safety and comfort. *Imperial War Museum*

These are German mountain troops identified by the Eidelweiss badge on the side of the cap. Their rifles are Mausers. They wear special boots and puttees wound round the legs.
Imperial War Museum

German infantryman in action at Verdun in France in 1940. He is firing a 7.92 mm MG 34 machine gun mounted on a bipod. This gun fired at a rate of 850 rounds a minute and used either a belt or a special twin cylinder saddle magazine. Note the wire fitted to his steel helmet which was used for securing camouflage netting.
Imperial War Museum

Although most people think of the Germans using nothing but tanks and other motor vehicles, they used a large number of horses. They were used to pull gun carriages and supply wagons as well as for patrolling and scouting as in this picture.
Imperial War Museum

Dogs and carrier pigeons were used as messengers by the German forces. Note the decal (transfer) of the national eagle holding the swastika mounted on the steel helmet. The shoulder strips were coloured to show the job of the wearer, i.e. infantry, cavalry and so on. On his right sleeve he has a yellow letter B for *Brieftaubenmeister* – Pigeon Post master. *Imperial War Museum*

Kuvelwagen – Kfz 1 – general purpose military car with folding top here being used in the deserts of North Africa 1941–2. Note the extra cans of petrol secured at the side near the back and the spare wheel carried on the bonnet.
Imperial War Museum

German army gas mask and carrying tin box. Inside the lid are gelatine patches which were used to prevent the glass eye pieces misting over when the mask was worn.

German infantry block a road with a steam roller. Their gas masks can be seen and many have stick grenades pushed down their boots ready for instant use.

Parade of German troops – the four men with the standards on the left wear the black Panzer uniform and beret which was later replaced by the ordinary pattern of cloth cap.

German troops in France 1940.
Note the breast eagle on the tunics and the water bottle carried on the right hip. The soldier at the rear is carrying a *Panzerbüchse* anti-tank gun.

German recruits at a training camp. The instructor wears a steel helmet and has a stripe on the arm of his tunic. The recruits wear the cloth cap known as a *Feldmutze*.

German officers in dress uniform pose for a group portrait with their swords. The centre officer has an Imperial German sword. The decoration on their collars shows the rank and the colour would show which branch of the service they were in.

German Lieutenant-Colonel – his cap has thin red piping to show he belongs to the artillery and his woven shoulder straps show his rank.
Imperial War Museum

Captured member of the famous German Afrika Korps who fought in North Africa. He wears a light sand coloured cap with the German eagle in pale blue. The long peak helped shade his eyes from the strong sun.

Two German infantrymen with their stick grenades. The one on the left is a Lance Corporal and the other is a Sergeant (*Feldwebel*) who has the Iron Cross and an Infantry Assault badge. He also has the M 1944 tunic which was much plainer than the earlier models – you can see that the breast pockets no longer have pleats.

This is a side cap worn by some members of the German Luftwaffe. The eagle and swastika badge was embroidered and the small circular badge was red, white and blue.
Martin Windrow

Italian Troops

Italian troops working on 90/53 mm Ausaldo anti-aircraft gun. They wear M 1935 steel helmets and their uniform was a grey-green in colour. *Imperial War Museum*

Italy ruled parts of Africa and so was able to use some of her native troops in the North African campaigns. Here some are firing a 12.7 M/G and each carries a Mannlicher-Carcano M 1891 rifle. *Imperial War Museum*

Many countries under Germany's control sent volunteers to help Hitler's forces when Russia was attacked. This is a patrol of Italians on the Russian front. The leader appears to be carrying a Beretta Model 1938A sub-machine gun.
Imperial War Museum

Japanese Troops

Japanese troops in action with their 7.7 mm Hotchkiss Mod. 92 machine gun adopted in 1932, with a rate of fire of only 450 rounds a minute. It was a very heavy weapon and consequently difficult to move in action. Note the sword held by the officer on the right. The Japanese were probably the last army to use their swords in action.
Imperial War Museum

Japanese troops in action in China, armed with the heavy Taisho 3 machine gun. It had a rather slow rate of fire and the tapping noise of its shots led the Allied troops to nickname it the Woodpecker. The cartridges were fed in from metal strips holding 30 rounds each.
Imperial War Museum

A Japanese steel helmet with its special long laces which were tied around the head in a rather unusual fashion to hold the helmet on. Most other armies had their helmets fitted with a chin-strap. The stencilled anchor suggests that this was either a naval or marine issue.

Small general purpose car used by the Japanese army – notice the star on the bonnet and the simple design of the wheels.
Imperial War Museum

British Troops

The North African campaigns involved many raids by troops working in small groups. This is a jeep of the Special Air Service Long Range Desert Group, one such British Unit. It is fitted with a .5 machine gun and a Vickers machine gun at the back. As these units often worked behind enemy lines they had to take plenty of supplies including water and petrol. The men's uniforms were often rather unusual. *Imperial War Museum*

Large numbers of Indian troops fought with the British forces during the war and here they parade in North Africa. Note the lanyard which goes round the neck and clips on to the butt of the revolver and so prevents its accidental loss. The troops are armed with Short Magazine Lee Enfield rifles.
Imperial War Museum

In the Ramu Valley in New Guinea a line of Commonwealth troops crosses the grassy plain. The troops have the wide brimmed hat like that worn by New Zealand and Australian troops which was adopted by many British troops serving in this theatre of war. Some wear their steel helmets complete with camouflage nets. Notice the mugs and bits carried on the back pack.
Imperial War Museum

A Sergeant of the British Airborne forces complete with parachute and heavy kit bags. He wears the special steel helmet with its extra straps and chin-pad. Note the special parachute badge on the stripes and the webbing anklets.
Imperial War Museum

British airborne troops, September 1944, wearing their maroon coloured berets with the large winged cap badge. They wear the loose camouflage jacket with its numerous pockets and the one second from the left is using a mess can instead of a mug for his tea. The planes in the background are US air force Dakotas.
Imperial War Museum

Military police in the British forces usually wore a red armband with the letters M.P. and in addition their belts, holsters and pouches were white. Here a group are parading in the slouch hat worn in the Far East. This group was part of the British Commonwealth Occupation Force (Japan) and wear a special badge on the shoulder of their tunic.

During 1940–41 many towns in Britain suffered from the German bombers. The men and women who dealt with the raids were members of the Air Raid Precautions force (ARP) and were identified by the white letter on their helmets – this is a Warden (W). He wears a blue overall and blows the whistle either to signal the approach of raiders or the all-clear. Note the special lining of the steel helmet and chin-strap with the spring section to keep it tight. *Imperial War Museum*

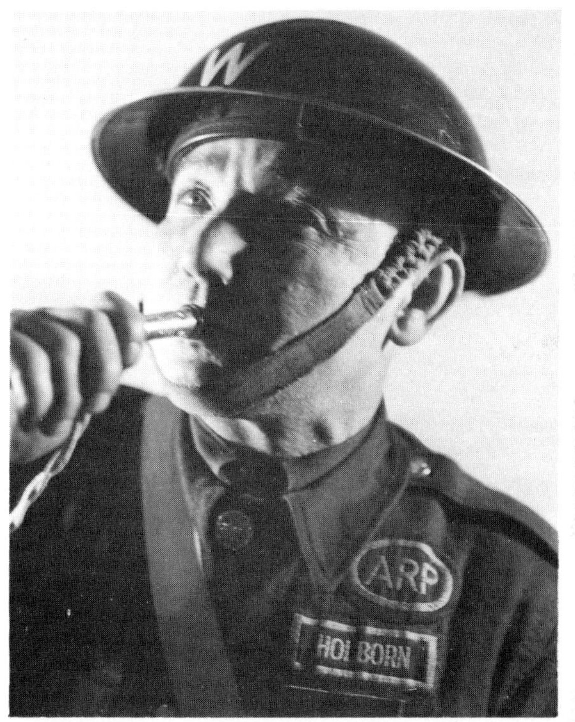

French Troops

A French cavalryman of 1940 with a bandoleer of cartridges across his shoulder. His uniform was khaki and the steel helmet a light, greyish blue colour.
Imperial War Museum

American Troops

US Paratroops of 17th Airborne Division at Mourmelon, France prepare for a jump. On their arms a large US flag is for identification. Note the dagger on the Sergeant's leg and the man on the left has a .45 Colt in a shoulder-holster just above his water bottle. They are busy strapping on a Thompson submachine gun.
Imperial War Museum

Russian Troops

The Cossacks of Russia have always been famous for their warlike character and wonderful riding. When Germany invaded Russia in 1942 some Cossacks joined the German army but most fought against the invaders. These two, father (Sgt.) and son (Lt.) are armed with the usual Russian sub-machine gun PPSh.
Imperial War Museum

Naval anti-aircraft gunners in action with the Russian Black Sea fleet. This and similar guns were designed to put up a massive curtain of fire against low-flying attacking aircraft. Note the Russian style steel helmet which was not unlike the US pattern. *Imperial War Museum*

The Russian army was one of the first to realize how useful parachute troops could be in battle. They tried them out in the 1930s. The first parachutes had the handle of the rip cord, which released the canopy or body of the chute, on the right-hand side. They wear a type of flying helmet rather than a special protective helmet like most other airborne forces.
Imperial War Museum

Solid brass buckle worn by some members of Soviet Russia's naval forces. The star has the hammer and sickle symbol found on many Russian items and stands for the workers of industry and agriculture.
F. J. Stephens

Medals

German Wound Badge given to any member of the armed forces .who was wounded in action. There were three classes, black, silver and gold. This is a silver, 2nd Class and was worn on the breast at the left-hand side of the tunic.
F. J. Stephens

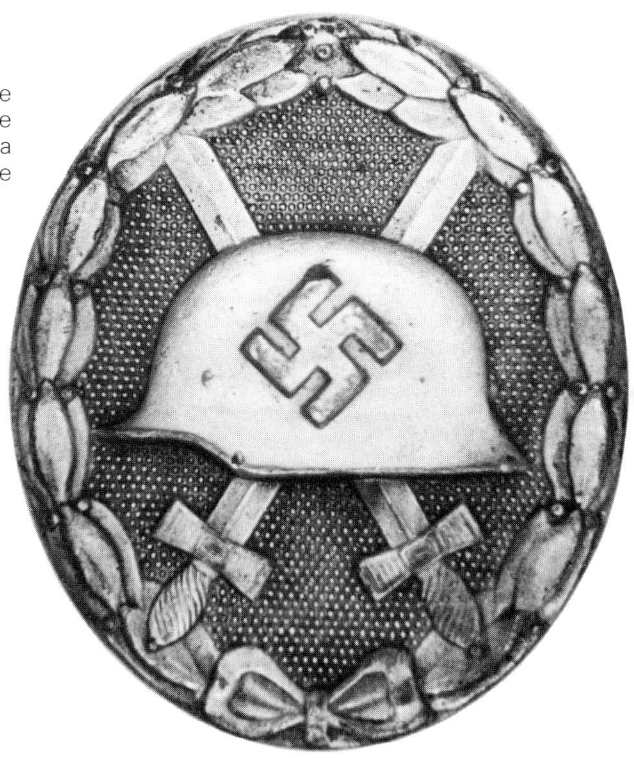

German War Merit crosses. Those with crossed swords were given to people who had performed some military service, those without swords were for civilians. The top one is a silver, 1st Class cross held on the coat by a pin. Left is a bronze, 2nd Class hung from a ribbon and on the right is a 2nd Class Civilian cross.
F. J. Stephens

Left: US Bronze Star Medal introduced in 1944 and awarded for operations against enemy on land or sea. (Ribbon red, white, blue, white, red)

Right: US Distinguished Flying Cross awarded for bravery in the air. (Ribbon blue, white, blue white, red, white, blue, white, blue)

US Distinguished Service Medal – awarded to members of the US army for bravery. (Ribbon red, blue and white)

US Purple Heart – awarded to anybody wounded in action. (Ribbon purple and white)

US Air Medal introduced in 1942 for service in the air. (Ribbon blue and orange)

US Asiatic-Pacific Campaign Medal for those who served in these campaigns between December 1941–March 1946.

German Iron Cross, 1st Class, worn on left breast pocket. The qualification needed to gain this medal was different for the various services.

British Africa Star awarded to those who served in North Africa between certain dates.

German Iron Cross, 2nd Class, with the blue envelope in which it was issued together with its length of ribbon.

Group of British World War II medals all issued without the owner's name.
Left to right: 1939–45 Star; Atlantic Star; Africa Star; Defence Medal; War Medal.

Other campaign medals which were awarded were Air Crew Europe Star, Pacific Star, Burma Star, Italy Star, France and Germany Star. Special medals were struck for Indian, Canadian, South African, Australian, New Zealand and Southern Rhodesian Forces.

108

Russian medal awarded for valour in action.

The most important of all British medals is the Victoria Cross which is only awarded for the most outstanding acts of bravery. During World War II only 152 Victoria Crosses were awarded.

Badges

Left to right:
Russian shoulder board – Captain of Infantry, gold and maroon.
Italian shoulder board – medium artillery, black and yellow.
British – red tab worn on collar of certain high-ranking officers.
Polish – green with eagle.

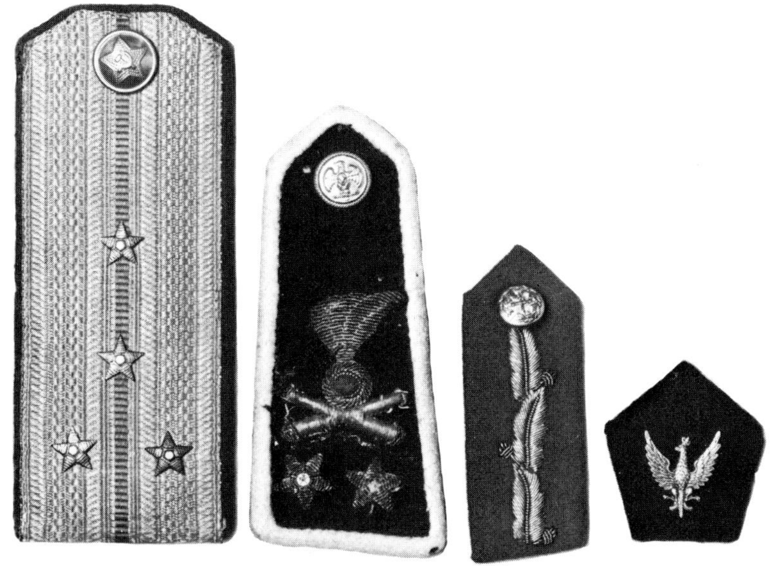

These R.A.F. cloth half-wings were worn above the left pocket.
1st line: Observer; Pilot
2nd line: Radio operator; bomb aimer
3rd line: Navigator; engineer
4th line: Aero engineer; signaller

Embroidered German Eagles
Top: Army enlisted men breast badge; Waffen SS arm badge.
Middle: Luftwaffe officer's breast badge.
Bottom: Army officer's cap eagle; Navy petty officer's cap eagle.

From top to bottom:
Embroidered arm eagle of the SS.
Small metal eagle worn on the cap.
German Luftwaffe breast badge for Ground Combat – first authorized in March 1942.
Metal Italian badge of Blackshirt brigade.
Metal Italian shoulder plate.

Top: Cap badge of Bulgarian officer.
Centre left: Cap badge of Czechoslovakian forces.
Centre right: Cap badge of Polish forces.
Bottom: Cap badge of Russian naval petty officer.

The different regiments of the British army were identified in many ways including the badge worn in the cap. These were originally made of metal but later during the war plastic was used.
Top: The Ayrshire (Earl of Carrick's Own) Yeomanry which served as a Field Regiment in the Royal Artillery.
Bottom left: The Carabiniers (6th Dragoon Guards).
Bottom right: The Duke of Lancaster's Own Yeomanry – served as Medium Regiment of the Royal Artillery.

The German armed forces awarded many badges for service in particular units and these were usually worn on the left breast pocket. This one was for service with Luftwaffe anti-aircraft batteries.

US Aircrew metal badges worn on the tunic above the left breast pocket.
Top to bottom: Service pilot; Glider pilot; Bombardier; Navigator; Shoulder patch of Airborne troop carrier.

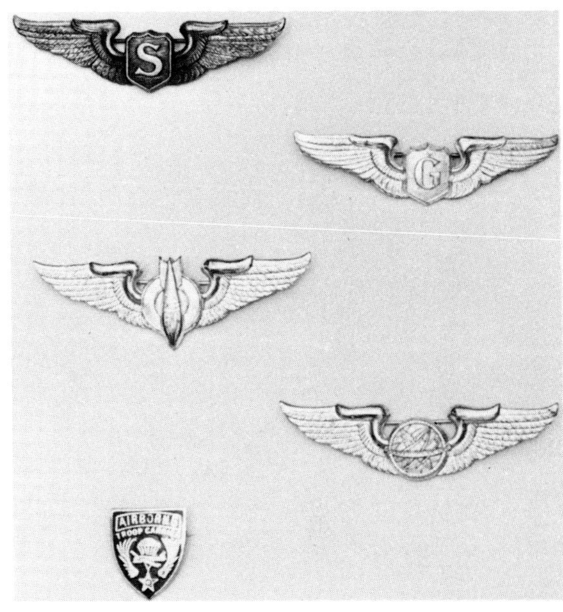

German shield badges awarded for service in various campaigns and usually worn on the top left arm of tunic.
Top left: Cholm Shield – a battle fought in Russia, January–March 1942.
Top right: Narvik Shield – the first of the shield badges granted for service at the battle of Narvik, Norway April–June 1940.
Centre: Demjansk Shield – another Russian battle 1941–2.
Bottom left: Crimea Shield – those who served in the Crimea September 1941–July 1942.
Bottom right: Kuban Shield – Russian battle begun in February 1943.

German flying clasp introduced in January 1941 and given to those who flew in bomber squadrons.

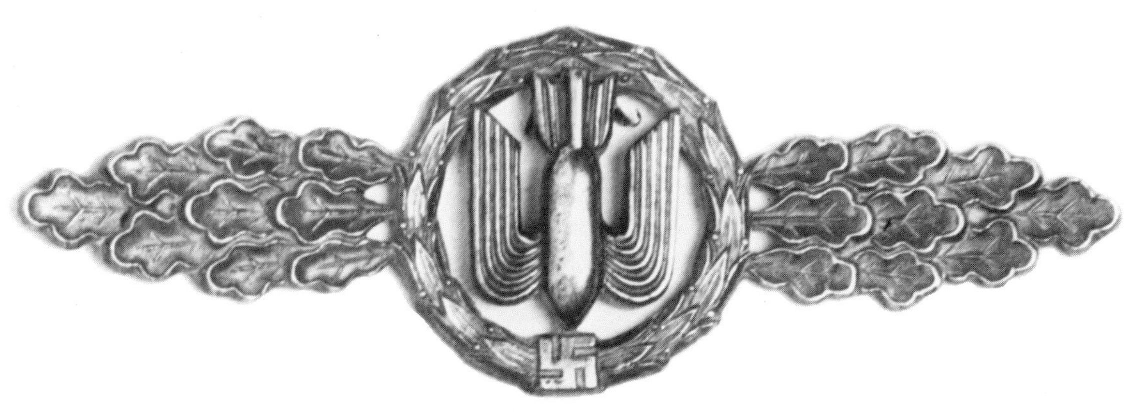

Canadian Cap Badges
Top left: 1st Battalion Canadian Scottish Regiment – made in white metal.
Top right: The Calgary Highlanders.
Bottom: The Cape Breton Highlanders.

Metal Eagles of Germany
Top: Waffen SS; Naval.
Middle: NSKK – Transport Corps.
Bottom: Luftwaffe N.C.O.'s peaked cap badge; Army.

Buttons

When the war started many British troops still had tunics with brass buttons but the blouse of the battledress became more common and this had ordinary, plain buttons. The R.A.F. tunic retained its brass buttons throughout most of the war.
Top left: Royal Corps of Signals.
Top right: Royal Artillery.
Bottom: Royal Air Force.

US buttons, cap and lapel badges – the one with crossed cannon was for Field Artillery troops, that with crossed pistols for the Military Police. The one with US was worn on the lapel by enlisted men.

Top: US Other ranks button with regimental number.

Bottom (left to right): Russian star; US Major's shoulder badge; Russian tank badge for a shoulder board.

German Car Flags

Many nations marked officers' cars by means of flags mounted on the wings. They were wired to make them stand out even when the car was stationary.

Index

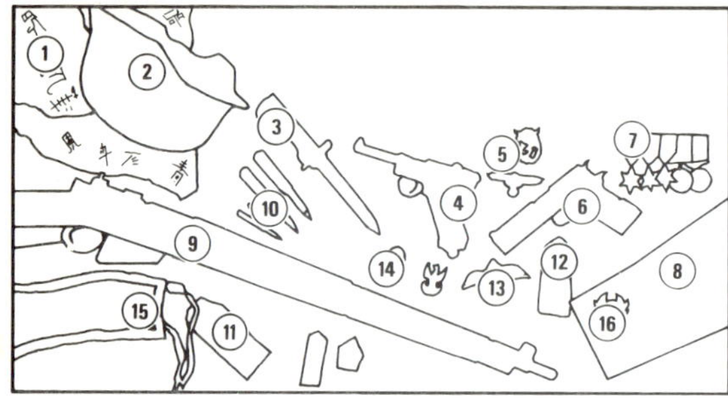

Jacket picture

1 Japanese flag with autographs of soldier's friends.
2 German Luftwaffe steel helmet.
3 US bayonet.
4 German '08 9 mm Luger automatic.
5 German Luftwaffe Ground Combat badge.
6 US .45 1911 A1 Colt automatic pistol.
7 Group of British campaign medals.
8 R.A.F. Flight Lieutenant's tunic.
9 British .303 No. 4 Mk 1 rifle.
10 Cartridges.
11 Russian shoulder board.
12 Italian shoulder board.
13 R.A.F. Pilot's badge.
14 Bulgarian Officer's cap badge.
15 British Air Raid Warden's arm band.
16 Russian naval cap badge.

Source Books

Aircraft
Commercial Vehicles
Dinghies
Hydrofoils and Hovercraft
Industrial Past
Locomotives
Military Support Vehicles
Military Tracked Vehicles
Motor Cars
Motorcycles
Naval Aircraft and Aircraft Carriers
Ships
Submarines and Submersibles
Tractors and Farm Machinery
Twentieth Century Warships
Underground Railways
Veteran Cars
Vintage and Post Vintage Cars
Windmills and Watermills
World War I Weapons and Uniforms